D0052992

Crochet
with Wire

Nancie M. Wiseman

Crochet with Wire

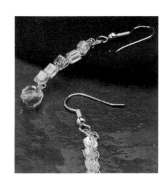
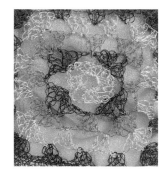
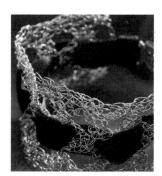

Nancie M. Wiseman

INTERWEAVE PRESS
www.interweave.com

Project editor: Christine Townsend
Technical editor: Karen Manthey, Ann Budd
Illustration: Gayle Ford
Photography: Joe Coca
Design: Paulette Livers, Dean Howes
Production: Dean Howes
Copy editor: Stephen Beal
Proofreader and Indexer: Nancy Arndt

Interweave Press, Inc.
201 East Fourth Street
Loveland, CO 80537 USA
www.interweave.com

Printed in Singapore by Tien Wah Press

Library of Congress Cataloging-in-Publication Data

Wiseman, Nancie, 1950-
  Crochet with wire / Nancie M. Wiseman.
     p. cm.
  Includes bibliographical references and index.
  ISBN 1-931499-77-2
  1. Crocheting. 2. Wire. 3. Jewelry making. I. Title.
  TT820.W615 2005
  746.43'4041--dc22
                              2004018417

10 9 8 7 6 5 4 3 2 1

Acknowledgments

I have many thanks to give many people for this book.

It's always a pleasure to work with the folks at Interweave Press. To all the editors, the designers, the magazine staff, bookkeepers, illustrators, warehouse folks, and everybody in between: You're a wonderful team, and it's great knowing you.

Artistic Wire, your generosity in donating the wire for all the projects in this book is unsurpassed. The colors made the projects a true joy to work on and develop—the problem for me was deciding which color to use! Thank you.

And, of course, my husband Bill—what would I do without you? You are so good to me, catering to my every need while I work on projects. I will always love you. Thank you for your help when I need it.

Thank you, Kay Holt and Laraine Jane Leadmon—two of my oldest and dearest friends. Kay sends e-mails that simply say "WRITE!" Laraine Jane (also known as G. J.) and I went to nursing school together and she sends e-mails to ask for knitting advice or just to say hello. She also keeps me updated on nursing stuff, because once it's in your blood, it's there to stay.

For the two dogs in my life, Amber, a golden retriever, and Pumpkin, a Yorkshire terrier, who sometimes provide my only exercise when I'm writing a book— I get up to open the door for them: Thanks, guys.

Contents

Introduction

Members of my family have been crocheting for generations. Long ago, of course, crocheting wasn't thought of as an art, but rather a necessity or, at best, a utilitarian pastime. As we moved through the industrial and electronic booms of the twentieth century and people gained leisure time, we saw more truly artful crochet designs in the likes of afghans, hats, shawls, and purses. Still, I'm sure my ancestors would be utterly shocked at the notion of crocheting with wire. I'd like to think, though, that they would revel in the lacy, glittering jewelry and the novel baskets.

I'm not certain whether it's the sparkle that catches my eye or because wire is so different from yarn, but I love working with wire—and beads. When I'm working with wire, it almost feels like I'm sculpting rather than crocheting. I'm creating and molding an enduring form.

Just how intricate the form becomes is up to you, but it's amazing how many stunning, whimsical, or functional jewelry and home decorator pieces you can make with basic crochet stitches. Most of the projects in this book are simple, requiring single crochet, half double crochet, and double crochet in the same basic patterns you use in yarn crochet. Some projects incorporate the more advanced techniques such as ripple stitch, filet crochet, Tunisian stitch, or adding beads as you work.

I hope you'll enjoy every minute you spend on these projects. They travel well; take them with you. All the how-to information about buying wire and beads, working with wire, and learning to crochet with wire is right here, so get your supplies lined up and get ready for a new form of crochet you won't be able to put down.

Wire, Glorious Wire

When I started crocheting with wire, I used copper wire from the hardware store. I didn't know much about wire then, but I knew this stuff was horrible. Hardware-store wire is used to wire lamps or stereos. It tarnishes and comes in only a few gauges—hard, harder, and way too hard. I'm surprised I even kept at it, but I was determined; I knew I could make the copper work, even while I dreamed of a more supple wire.

Those dreams dictated my search for softer, better quality wire on the Internet, in bead magazines, and at bead stores. Fortunately, it was about this time that wireworking was becoming quite popular with people who, like me, did beadwork. I was hoping to find gold, silver, or copper wire, but I found colors, too. Oh, what fun this new technique was going to be!

The next step was to determine which gauge, or thickness, of wire would work for crochet. Would I have to stick with one, or could I experiment with several? I could tell just by looking at some of the gauges that they were too thick, so I ruled them out immediately. Some of the midrange gauges were what I was looking for, but because wire workers didn't use them, they were hard to find in the stores. I bought some 26- and 28-gauge wire to play with and discovered that they were pretty easy to work.

Let me explain about gauges right now, so the numbers make sense. The lower the number of the gauge, the thicker the wire. You can get very heavy 12-gauge wire, which is what some wire workers like to pound with a hammer and shape, or you can get wire as fine as 34 gauge, which is nearly as fine as a hair from your head. Somewhere in the middle there is the easiest range to work with for those of us who want to crochet and not pound with a hammer. My lower limit is 26 gauge; it's pretty stiff but still works. My upper limit is 34 gauge; once it is crocheted it gains strength and looks like gossamer stitches. I consider 28 and 30 gauge perfect for crochet. It all takes some getting used to, but the "getting used to" is part of the fun!

As I continued my search for wire, I found Artistic Wire (see Resources, page 87), which is what I use the most. It is available in most bead stores, craft stores, catalogs, and of course, on the Internet. It is permanently coated copper wire and comes in an amazing array of colors. It doesn't tarnish, and Artistic Wire has a new process for making silvered wire that gives it an incredible shine and sparkle. Artistic Wire is very reasonably priced, too. The widest range of colors is available in 26, 28, and 30 gauge; there are fewer colors in the thicker and thinner gauges. There is plenty of yardage on a spool for a

project, unless you use the silvered wire, which has less yardage.

You'll need some wire just to noodle around with and get the feel of before you start a project. Start with some 28-gauge wire and a size B (2.25 mm) crochet hook and experiment with single crochet, half double crochet, and double crochet. You don't need to make anything; stick to a sampler of the stitches until you get the feel of what it's like to work with the wire instead of working with yarn. If you're new to crochet, begin with yarn to become familiar with the stitches before you attempt them with wire (see pages 19 to 20 for more information on crochet stitches).

Sterling silver wire is also available by the ounce from Rio Grande in Albuquerque, New Mexico (see Resources, page 87). To make an economical order you'll need to know exactly how much wire you need, but it's fabulous to work with and worth the investment. It comes in limited gauges and some-

times feels a bit stiffer to work with than Artistic Wire, but it will certainly make a treasure to last a lifetime.

There are other brands of wire that would work for wire crochet, but I haven't experimented with them. Whatever brand of wire you use, first do research on it: Make sure it doesn't tarnish and comes in the gauges and colors you want. And be sure it's good enough wire so that after you've put in all the work to make a lovely necklace or basket, the finish won't scrape off the wire and ruin the piece.

Tools for Wire Crochet

Crochet Hooks

The size of the hooks used in the projects for this book varies from a size 7 (1.65 mm) steel crochet hook up to a size E (3.50 mm) crochet hook. There is a vast difference in these sizes; the steel crochet hooks are the smallest and those categorized by letters are the largest (see the charts, right). Steel crochet hooks are used mostly with crochet thread and lettered crochet hooks are used mostly with yarn. If you haven't done much crochet with thread you may need to practice with the smaller hooks a little before you use them with wire. Using them isn't hard; it's just that the work is on such a tiny scale.

MODIFIED LIST OF CROCHET HOOK SIZES

Millimeter equivalent may vary slightly from manufacturer to manufacturer.

Lettered Crochet Hook Sizes

Size	mm equivalent
B	2.25
C	2.75
D	3.25
E	3.50
F	3.75
G	4.25

Steel Crochet Hook Sizes

Size	mm equivalent
1	2.75
2	2.25
3	2.10
4	2.00
5	1.90
6	1.80
7	1.65
8	1.50

I prefer metal crochet hooks for crocheting with wire because it's just too rough on wood or plastic hooks. Experiment and see what you think. You may find that your old hooks work just fine, whatever they are.

I love the new crochet hooks because their wide grip provides good leverage for working with heavy wire. You'll probably find that the hooks you prefer to use for thread or yarn are the ones you'll like best for crocheting with wire.

Chain-Nose Pliers

Chain-nose pliers resemble regular pliers, but they have no teeth on the surface of the gripping area to ruin the surface of the wire. They are good pliers for attaching findings, wire wrapping, and finishing off pieces crocheted with wire.

Rolling Pin

Some crochet pieces require "blocking" to strengthen them. A regular baker's rolling pin used on a flat surface covered by newspaper works perfectly. Gently move the rolling pin over the surface of the work in the direction it was crocheted.

Wire Cutters

You'll find wire cutters in most bead, craft, and hobby stores. Choose wire cutters that are lightweight and have easy-grip coated handles. The cutting end has a flat side and an angled side. Position the flat side toward the work to get a straight cut; position the angled side toward the work for an angled cut. For safety purposes, I use only the flat side and make only straight cuts because the edge of a flat cut is not as sharp as an angled cut. Never use wire cutters to cut anything but wire.

Wire Smoother

Wire smoothers look like heavy-duty pliers but have a nylon-covered jaw to smooth kinked or twisted wire. Crocheting with wire can create little snafus that make this tool invaluable in your toolbox.

How to Crochet with Wire

The great news is that the basic crochet stitches are the same whether you work with wire or with yarn, although working with wire feels a bit different and you may have to tug and pull a little harder, especially with heavy gauges. Working with fine-gauge wire feels similar to working with fine crochet thread, but you may find it difficult to pull the stitches as tight as you are used to doing with thread crochet; moreover, the stitches are a little harder to see for subsequent rows. It takes some practice to get the feel of working on fine wire with small hooks, but it's similar to getting the feeling of switching from worsted-weight yarn to size 10 crochet thread. Just take your time and get the feel of the small wires and hooks with a few practice pieces before you leap into a large project.

How to Hold the Wire and Hook

You may find you won't be able to wrap wire in your fingers as you do yarn. If you try, the wire will tighten up too much and may actually hurt your hands. Since it doesn't stretch, wire doesn't require as much tension as yarn. Experiment with different ways of holding the wire in the hand you don't crochet with. You may find that one wrap around your index finger is all that's needed.

Fine-gauge wires can cut into the skin if you aren't careful (keep in mind that fine wire is used in cheese cutters)! The best thing to do when you're crocheting with fine wire is to relax—just as you do when you're crocheting with fine threads and let the wire flow from the spool into your hand. You may be inclined to try some new way of holding the wire to make it feel just right, but the truth is that it may always feel a bit different. Here's a tip: Put plenty of lotion or cream on your hands to keep the wire flowing smoothly and to protect your cuticles.

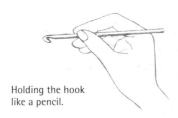

Holding the hook like a pencil.

Holding the hook like a knife.

I have always held my crochet hook with my hand under the hook—like I was holding a pencil—but with some of the heavier wires, I've found that I have to hold my hand over the hook—like I was holding a knife for more leverage. Doing so felt strange because, for me, it was such a different way to hold the hook, but being willing to experiment is one key to successful wire crocheting.

Stringing Beads

If a project calls for stringing beads before you start crocheting, you'll be delighted by the fact that most wire is usually heavy and stiff enough to act as a beading needle you can string the beads on the wire without extra tools or accessories. Pour the beads into a small dish, dip the wire into the dish, and string on the beads.

If the wire is too fine to act as a stringing needle, a sewing needle with an eye large

Use a wire or needle to pick up beads to string.

Put beads in a small bowl to keep them contained.

enough to accommodate the wire yet slim enough to string beads is a great tool. I use a size 10 quilting needle, but a small sewing needle works well as long as it can accept the wire and then a bead going over the wire folded through its eye. Here's a tip: I've learned from experimentation that the eye on most beading needles is too small for wire, so don't even bother trying them.

Getting the Kinks Out

If the wire gets kinked as you work, you can run your fingers over it to straighten it, or you can gently pull on both sides of the kink and rub the wire against the edge of a table. Don't manipulate the wire too much or it is likely to break. Or use a wire smoother (see tools, page 13). Holding the wire in one hand, run the smoother down the wire several times. You'll find that it isn't necessary to get the kinks out completely because once the wire is crocheted you won't be able to see them.

I've discovered that when I crochet with beads, the wire doesn't kink; the beads seem to keep the wire straight. So even when your project doesn't require beads, place four or five medium-sized seed beads (or one large bead) on the wire just to keep it from kinking. As you work, push the beads down out of the way; you'll find that using beads won't slow your progress, but it can save you a lot of grief. Remove the beads when you've finished the project and cut the wire. Cut the wire when you've finished the project and remove the bead.

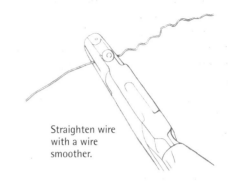

Straighten wire with a wire smoother.

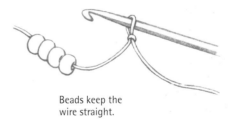

Beads keep the wire straight.

Wire Crochet with Beads

All beads must be prestrung on the wire
before you begin crocheting. In some cases
the order of the beads is random, but in
others the order is very specific: This
information is given in the directions for
each project. Be very careful when you
string beads in a certain order; if you make
a mistake, you may have to start over
to correct it.

Once you've strung all the beads for
a project, let them slide down the
wire but not too far. As you need
them, simply reach down and pull
the next bead up to where it is to
be used and work the next
stitch as directed. I think
it's fascinating to watch
the beads fall into place
as you work the stitch-
es. When you make a
chain stitch with beads
they will dominate the whole
chain. When you work single
crochet, beads slip into position
on wrong-side rows so that they
appear on the right side of the work.

When you're placing beads, be sure your
stitches are firm enough to keep the beads
in place. Doing so takes some getting used
to since wire doesn't stretch. You may want
to try a practice piece before you start for

real. And don't forget the most important advice: Relax and enjoy the fun!

Basic Stitches

These are the basic stitches used to crochet with wire. Abbreviations are listed in parentheses.

SLIPKNOT

Make a loop, and then pull another loop through it with your fingers or the crochet hook. Tighten gently on the hook.

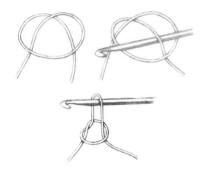

CHAIN STITCH (CH ST)

Make a slipknot (see slipknot, page 20) on hook. Yarn over hook and draw it through the loop of the slipknot on the crochet hook. Do not tighten the stitch on the crochet hook. Repeat, drawing through the last loop formed.

CHAIN STITCH WITH BEADS

Drop a bead next to the loop on the hook, yarn over hook, and pull the loop through the stitch on the hook. Repeat for as many stitches as required in the project.

SINGLE CROCHET (SC)

Insert hook into an edge stitch, yarn over hook and draw a loop through, yarn over hook (Figure 1) and draw it through both loops on hook (Figure 2).

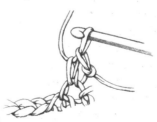

Figure 1

Figure 2

SINGLE CROCHET WITH BEAD

Drop a bead next to the loop on hook, insert hook into the next stitch, yarn over hook and draw a loop through, yarn over hook and draw it through the two remaining loops on hook.

HALF DOUBLE CROCHET (HDC)

Yarn over hook, insert hook into a stitch, yarn over hook and draw a loop through stitch (three loops on hook), yarn over hook (Figure 1) and draw it through all loops on the hook (Figure 2).

Figure 1

Figure 2

DOUBLE CROCHET (DC)

Yarn over hook, insert the hook into a stitch, yarn over hook and draw a loop through (three loops on hook); yarn over hook (Figure 1) and draw it through two loops, yarn over hook and draw it through the remaining two loops (Figure 2).

Figure 1

Figure 2

Attaching Closures, Fastening, and Finishing Off

Although it may not make much sense in the beginning, it can be fun to plan the finishing before you start a project. Sometimes part of a closure can be attached with the first chain stitch. If you think ahead and plan the type of closure you're going to use, that choice often provides direction for the overall design.

It's true, though, that you may not make a decision about the closure until you finish the piece. That's usually what happens in my designs—I may not be quite sure just how they are going to end and how heavy or what type of a closure I will want, so I make the decision after I'm finished.

No matter how you proceed with a creation, always be sure you leave long-enough tails on either end. Sometimes you use tails to sew or secure the closures to the crochet. About 8" (20.5 cm) is enough for the wire to be easy to work with and finish into the stitches.

Closures

You can find a wonderful variety of closures (these are included in the larger bead category called findings) to augment the beauty of pieces. Most are simple to attach by sewing or using jump rings. Here are examples of a few and how to attach them to the crochet.

FILIGREE BOX CLASPS

Best attached to flat ends of jewelry, these clasps usually have two to three holes on each piece and need to be sewn to each side of the necklace or bracelet. Use wire tail ends to attach them.

HOOKS

Like the hooks and eyes used on clothing, one piece typically has a hook shape and the other has a loop to catch the hook. Attach one piece to each end of the necklace with the wire tail ends. Don't use hooks on bracelets; they're not secure.

JUMP RINGS

Jump rings are wire circles used as connectors. I caution you: You cannot squeeze the gap between the two ends of a jump ring tight enough to keep just one strand of wire from wiggling out of it. Always be sure that a jump ring goes through many strands of wire when it is attached. You can also use the end of the wire to sew into the jump ring several times so it can't wiggle out of the crochet.

LOBSTER CLAWS

Lobster claws are secure clasps, usually attached with a jump ring on one end of a necklace or bracelet, and always attached to a jump ring on the other end.

MAGNETIC CLASPS

These wonderful clasps work well for connecting lightweight jewelry. Crochet-wire necklaces and bracelets are perfect for magnetic clasps because most are very lightweight. Join magnetic clasps to wire crochet with tails ends attached to jump rings.

BAR AND RING TOGGLE CLASP

These clasps connect by slipping a bar on one end through a ring on the other. Although they are easy to sew on with the ends of wire, be sure that the toggle bar has enough room to wiggle so it can be easily manipulated for donning the necklace or bracelet.

Fastening Off: Weaving in Ends and Cutting

Wire that has been crocheted isn't likely to unravel, but don't just cut it off close to where you finished. Weave in the ends through a few stitches to give the piece structural integrity and, since the ends won't show, a polished finish.

Here are some rules to follow for cutting wire:

• Always wear eye protection.

• If possible, weave the wire into a bead a couple of times and cut the wire close to where it comes out of the bead.

• Cut over a garbage can and watch where the wire ends fly. These ends are very sharp, dangerous to small children and animals, and aren't pleasant to step on with bare feet. Dispose of all stray ends immediately.

• Be sure to use the flat side of the wire cutters.

• Always cut the wire away from the side that will be worn next to the skin.

• Check—and check again—that you are cutting the right piece of wire.

Projects

SKILL LEVELS

I use the most recent definitions from the Craft Yarn Council to designate the skill level of the patterns in this book. These levels are those that apply to garments, afghans, and yarn crochet in general, and they apply to wire crochet, too. They'll help you select the projects that are perfect for you.

Beginner: Projects for first-time crocheters that use basic stitches. Minimal shaping.

Easy: Projects that use yarn or thread with basic stitches, repetitive stitch patterns, simple color changes, simple shaping, and finishing.

Intermediate: Projects that use a variety of techniques, such as basic lace patterns or color patterns, mid-level shaping, and finishing.

Experienced: Projects with intricate stitch patterns, techniques, and dimensions, such as nonrepeating patterns, multicolor techniques, fine threads, small hooks, detailed shaping, and refined finishing.

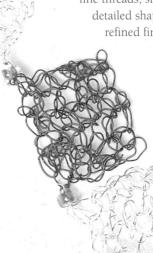

Off the Cuff

Skill Level
Easy

Finished Size
½" × 8" (1.3 cm × 20.5 cm)

Materials
- *Wire:* Artistic Wire, 28-gauge (15 yd [14 m] spool); 1 spool of natural copper
- *Beads:* 60 to 70 irregularly shaped agates about ⅜" (1 cm)
- *Hook:* Steel size 4/2.00 mm
- *Notions:* Wire cutter

Easy to slip on and off, this cuff is a snap to make and an absolute joy to wear. You'll want to make one to match every outfit in your closet!

String agates on wire. Make a ch 8" (20.5 cm) long, chaining an agate in each st. Join with a sl st in first ch, being careful not to twist the ch.

Rnd 1: Ch 2, hdc in each st around, join with a sl st, turn.

Rnd 2: Ch 1, sc an agate in each st around, join with a sl st in first sc. Fasten off.

FINISHING
Weave in ends, finish off in a bead, and cut close to work. The cuff will stretch slightly to go over the widest part of the hand and onto the wrist.

Leaf Cuff

So green and light, you'll love making—and wearing—the Leaf Cuff.

Skill Level
Easy

Finished Size
½" × 8½" (1.3 cm × 21.5 cm)

Materials
- *Wire:* Artistic Wire, 30-gauge (15 yd [14 m] spool); 1 spool of chartreuse
- *Beads:* 75 green glass leaves, ½" (1.3 cm) long 75 size 8° green seed beads to match leaves
- *Hook:* Steel size 6/1.80 mm
- *Notions:* Wire cutters

Note: Stretch cuff slightly after each row.

String beads on wire: Start with a leaf and alternate with a bead, ending with a bead. Make a ch 8½" (21.5 cm) long, ch a bead or a leaf in each st, being sure to end with a leaf. Join with a sl st in first ch, being careful not to twist ch.

Rnd 1: Ch 2, (sk st with bead, sc in st with leaf, ch 1), join across with sl st in first sc, turn.

Rnd 2: Ch 1, (sc a bead over a st with a leaf, sc a leaf over a st with a bead), join across with a sl st in first sc, turn.

Rnd 3: Ch 1, (sc in st with leaf, ch 1, sk st with bead), join with sl st, turn.

Rnd 4: Rep Rnd 2.
Fasten off.

FINISHING
Weave in ends, finish off in a bead, and cut close to work. Stretch the bracelet slightly to go over the hand.

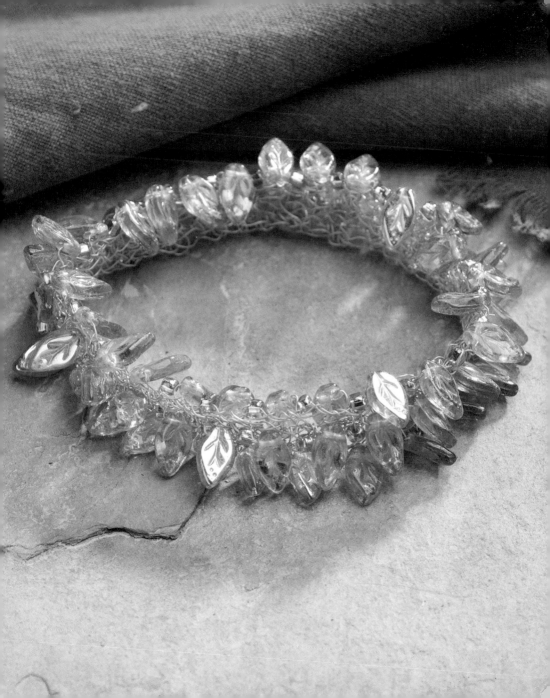

Central Bead with Wire Ribbon

Using any flat piece of blown or dichroic glass, you can crochet a simple necklace to match the colors of the glass. It works best if the back of the glass is flat and has a slit for an opening. The dichroic glass in this piece measures 1½" by ½" (3.8 cm × 1.3 cm) at its widest point.

Skill Level
Easy

Finished Size
⅜" × 22" (1 cm × 56 cm) with clasp

Materials
- *Wire:* Artistic Wire, 30-gauge (30 yd [28 m] spool); 1 spool each of the following colors:
  Color A: lemon
  Color B: turquoise
- *Beads:* Blown glass or dichroic glass with slit through the back for center piece
- *Hook:* Steel size 6/1.80 mm
- *Notions:* Gold clasp (clasp should be flat to match the style of the necklace)
  Wire cutters

Row 1: Insert color A wire into bead. Let the bead slide down, go back to the beg of the wire and ch 75 , move bead up to last ch, ch 1 around bead, ch 76.

Row 2: Turn, sc in second ch and in each ch to bead, sc into ch around bead, and in each ch to end. Finish off.

Row 3: *Insert color B wire into bead. Join to top edge of color A with a sl st, sc into each color A st across, sc around bead, and cont across rem sts of color A. Finish off.*

Row 4: Repeat from * to * with color B on opposite side of color A.

Smooth the crochet between your fingers. Cut a piece of wire and reinforce the crochet through the bead by sewing through the bead and into the crochet several times.

FINISHING
Sew clasp to ends of necklace with remaining wire tail ends. Weave in ends, finish off, and cut close to work.

Central Bead with Beaded Chain

Once you've found a showcase central bead for this necklace, you'll love working the chain with just the perfect seed beads to show it off. This is an easy project, but once you're finished, you're sure to get compliments every time you wear it.

Skill Level
Easy

Finished Size
20" (51 cm) with clasp

Materials
- *Wire:* Artistic Wire, 30-gauge (30 yd [28 m] spool); 1 spool of gold
- *Beads:* Central bead about 1¼" × ¾" (3.2 × 2 cm) with a large hole running lengthwise through the middle

  5 g size 8° triangular seed beads, brass
- *Hook:* Steel size 7/1.65 mm
- *Notions:* 1" (2.5 cm) gold toggle clasp

  4 gold crimp beads

  Wire cutters

  Needle-nose pliers

String about 30" (76 cm) of beads on wire. String the large bead over the strung seed beads. It must be able to move freely over the seed beads.

Row 1: Make a ch 9" (23 cm) long, ch a bead into each st. Move the large bead up to the last st and crochet the large bead into the next st by making a very large ch. Make a ch 9" (23 cm) long, ch a bead into each st for the other side. Cut wire. Fasten off.

Rows 2–4: Rep Row 1 (3 times).

Row 5: String about 30" (76 cm) of beads on wire. String the large bead over the strung seed beads. Make a ch 9" (23 cm) long, ch a bead into each st. String the large bead over the strung seed beads. Ch 1 over large bead, turn, ch 1. Gather all strands of wire on top of bead from ch sts of previous rows, work 9 sc over all of the wires, join to the opposite side with a sl st. Ch 1, turn, sc in each of next 9 sc, ch a bead into each st, join with a sl st. Make a ch 9" (23 cm) long, ch a bead into each st. Cut wire, fasten off.

Crimp Bead

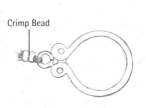

Clasp with a crimp bead.

FINISHING

Straighten out all the chains and trim to equal length. Place 2 crimp beads over the ends of the wire at one end. Place one side of the toggle clasp over the same pieces of wire, fold the wire over and reinsert into the crimp beads. Crimp the beads tightly with needle-nose pliers. Trim excess wire. Repeat for other side.

Squares Necklace

Dare to be square! For this necklace, each square is crocheted separately then joined with a bead to the adjacent square. The beaded chain added to the back makes the necklace adjustable for any neckline.

Skill Level
Intermediate

Finished Size
⅞" × 18" (2.2 cm × 5.5 cm) with clasp

Materials
- *Wire:* Artistic Wire, 28-gauge (30 yd [28 m] spool); 1 spool each of the following colors:
  Color A: silver
  Color B: peacock blue
  Artistic Wire, 28-gauge (15 yd [14 m] spool), 1 spool color C, plum
- *Beads:* 80 size 5° triangular clear mauve beads
- *Hooks:* Steel sizes 6 (1.80 mm) and 8 (1.50 mm)
- *Notions:* Silver-colored hook for clasp Wire cutters

Before you begin, use color A wire to thread the hook clasp followed by 20 beads. Let the beads slide down and out of the way until you need them.

Square 1: Using color C wire and size 6 (1.80 mm) hook, ch 6.

Row 1: Sc in second ch from hook, sc in each of next 4 ch, turn—5 sts.

Rows 2–6: Ch 1, sc in each st across, turn.

Cut wire, do not fasten off (Figure 1). Remove the hook from the loop.

Place a bead on the size 8 (1.50 mm) hook, insert the hook through the loop and slightly elongate the loop, slide the bead over the loop (Figure 2), remove the hook and reinsert the size 6 (1.8 mm) hook in the loop, pull up a loop of color A (next color Figure 3). Pull on the two tails to make sure the loop is small and even within the bead. Twist the two tails together to secure. This twist will be removed later when the ends are woven in.

Figure 1. Size 6 hook in last stitch.

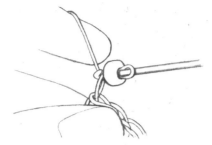

Figure 2. Size 8 hook with
bead, slide over the hook.

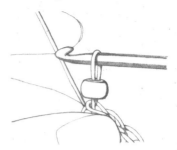

Figure 3. Size 6 hook placed
back in loop to begin new color.

Square 2: Using color A, rep Square 1, join
color B.

Square 3: Using color B, rep Square 1, join
color A.

Square 4: Using color A, rep Square 1, join
color C.

Square 5: Using color C, rep Square 1, join
color A.

Square 6: Using color A, rep Square 1, join
color B.

Square 7: Using color B, rep Square 1, join
color A.

Square 8: Using color A, rep Square 1, join
color C.

Square 9: Using color C, rep Square 1, join
color A.

Using color A, work 20, ch a bead with
each st until you reach the hook clasp. Ch
the clasp hook into the last st. Cut the wire
and overcast (by sewing with the wire as
though it were sewing thread) around the
hook several times to secure. Weave the wire
into the beads and fasten off.

String all the remaining beads except 6 on
color A. Join with a sl st to the opposite end
of the necklace, work a ch with a bead in
each st until 4 beads rem. Draw up 4 beads,
work a ch with the 4 beads, fasten off leaving
a 12" (30.5 cm) tail. Sew the remaining
beads one at a time into the 4-bead st to
make a larger bead. Weave the wire into the
beads and fasten off.

Bead Encrusted Necklace and Bracelet

Here's a fabulous necklace and bracelet totally encrusted with beads and charms made with—believe it or not—simple single crochet. It's what you choose for embellish- ment that makes the set fun to crochet and even more fun to wear. The clasp on this necklace is so beautiful, I'd wear it on the front.

Skill Level
Easy

Finished Size
Necklace: ½" × 17" (1.3 cm × 43 cm) with clasp
Bracelet: ⅞" × 7½" (2.2 cm × 19 cm) with clasp

Materials for Necklace
- *Wire:* Artistic Wire, 28-gauge (40 yd [37 m] spool); 1 spool of navy or color of your choice
- *Beads:* 250 to 300 beads, mixture including: Size 6° and 8° seed beads to match wire Charms of your choice 6 crystals, 8mm, and larger beads in flower and leaf shapes; string all beads on wire
- *Hook:* Steel size 4/2.00 mm
- *Notions:* Sterling silver flower toggle clasp from Fire Mountain Gems and Beads Wire cutters

Materials for Bracelet
- *Wire:* Artistic Wire, 28-gauge (15 yd [14 m] spool); 1 spool of purple or color of your choice to match beads
- *Beads:* 100 to 110 (or more for longer bracelet) beads, mixture including: Size 6° and 8° seed beads Charms 6 crystals, 8mm and larger beads in flower and leaf shapes; string all beads on wire
- *Hook:* Steel size 4/2.00 mm
- *Notions:* Silver filigree clasp Wire cutters

Notes: Work all single crochets through both loops. It is not necessary to sc a bead into a stitch with every stitch if the row looks too crowded. If too much wire shows, you can also sc 2 small beads into a single stitch.

Necklace

Row 1: (RS) Ch 5, sc in second ch from
　　hook, and in each ch across, turn—4 sts.
Row 2: (bead placement row) Ch 1, sc a bead
　　in each st across, turn.
Row 3: Ch 1, sc in each st across, turn.
　Rep Rows 2 and 3 until bracelet measures
16" (40.5 cm) or desired length; end with
Row 3. Fasten off.

FINISHING

Sew on clasp with tails of wire remaining at
both ends.

Bracelet

Row 1: (WS) Ch 4, sc in second ch from
　　hook, and in each ch across, turn—3 sts.
Row 2: Ch 1, 2 sc in each st across, turn—6
　　sts.
Row 3: (Bead placement row) Ch 1, sc a
　　bead into each st across, turn.
Row 4: Ch 1, sc in each st across, turn.
　Rep Rows 3 and 4 until bracelet measures
6½" (16.5 cm) or desired length; end with
Row 4. No more beads are placed.
Next row: Ch 1, (sk 1 st, sc in next st) across
　　row, turn—3 sts.
Next row: Ch 1, sc across, turn.
Next row: Ch 1, sk first 2 sts, sc in last st.
　　Fasten off.

FINISHING

Sew on clasp with tails of wire remaining at
both ends.

Silver and Crystals Necklace, Bracelet, and Earrings

Fit for a bride or made for a queen, this beautiful set is sure to be the crowning glory of any special occasion.

Skill Level

Easy

Finished Size

Necklace: ½" × 18½" (1.3 cm × 47 cm) with clasp

Bracelet: ¾" × 9" (2 cm × 23 cm)

Earrings: 2½" (6.5 cm) each with ear wire

Materials for Necklace

- *Wire:* Artistic Wire, 30-gauge (30 yd [28 m] spool); 1 spool of silver
- *Beads:* 13 clear 8mm crystals
  26 clear 3.5mm square beads
  39 clear 8mm seed beads
- *Hook:* Steel size 6/1.80 mm
- *Notions:* 2 small safety pins
  Silver or pewter clasp
  Wire cutters

Materials for Bracelet

- *Wire:* Artistic Wire, 30-gauge (30 yd [28 m] each spool); 1 spool of silver
- *Beads:* 9 clear 8mm clear crystals
  86 clear 3.5mm clear square beads
- *Hook:* Steel size 6/1.80 mm
- *Notions:* Wire cutters
  Chain-nose pliers

Materials for Earrings

- *Wire:* Artistic Wire, 30-gauge (30 yd [28 m] spool); 1 spool of silver (or leftovers from necklace and bracelet)
- *Beads:* 10 clear 3.5mm square beads
  2 clear 8mm crystals
- *Hook:* Steel size 6/1.80 mm
- *Notions:* 2 silver fishhook ear wires
  2 silver jump rings
  Wire cutters
  Chain-nose pliers

Necklace

Thread beads on wire in this order: *Crystal (size 8mm seed bead, 3.5mm square bead) twice, size 8mm seed bead. Repeat from * 12 more times.

Make a ch 19" (48.5 cm) long.

Row 1: (RS) Sc in second ch from hook and in each ch across, turn.

Row 2: Mark the center 43 sts with a safety pin at each end. Ch 1, sc to first st with safety pin, *(Ch 1 with 8mm seed bead, ch 1 with square bead) twice, ch 1 with 8mm seed bead, ch 1 with crystal, turn, sl st up WS of ch to top of ch, sc in next 7 sts of necklace; rep from * 6 more times, sc in each st of necklace to end of row, turn. *Note:* Last chain of beads should have been placed at last safety pin. Keep all chains with beads to RS of work.

Row 3: Ch 1, sc to center st between 1 st and second bead fringe, *(ch 1 with 8mm seed bead, ch 1 with square bead) twice, ch 1 with 8mm seed bead, ch 1 with crystal, turn, sl st up WS of ch to top of ch, sc in next 7 sts of necklace; rep from * 5 more times, sc in each st of necklace to end of row, turn.

Row 4: Ch 1, sc across. Fasten off.

FINISHING

Smooth with fingers to block. Sew on clasp
with tails of wire remaining at both ends.

Bracelet

Thread beads on wire in this order: 43
clear 3.5mm square beads, 9 clear 8mm
crystals, and 43 clear 3.5mm square beads.

Ch 44 sts, placing a square bead with each
of the first 43 sts.

Row 1: (WS) Sc in second ch from hook and
in each ch across, turn—43 sts.

Row 2: Ch 1, sc in each st across, turn.

Row 3: Ch 1, sc with crystal in first st sc in
next 2 sts, (sc with crystal in next st, sc in
next 5 sts) 6 times, sc with crystal in next
st, sc to last st, sc with crystal in last st,
turn.

Row 4: Ch 1, sc in each st across, turn.

Row 5: Ch 1, sc with square bead in each st
across. Fasten off.

FINISHING

Using remaining ends of wire, sew two short
ends of bracelet together.

Earrings

Thread beads on wire in this order: 5 clear
3.5mm square beads and 1 clear 8mm crystal.

Ch 5, sc a bead into each stitch. Ch 1,
placing the crystal, and pulling the last st up
toward the chain.

FINISHING

Attach ear wires using a jump ring in loop at
the end furthest away from the crystal.
Weave in end.

Winter Trees Necklace and Earrings

Doesn't this necklace remind you of the starkness of winter trees with bright sparkly white lights wrapped around the limbs? I've included several other options for color combinations: Green wire with multicolor beads for a Christmas tree; gold wire with leaves and beads in copper colors for autumn; and for spring, green wire with lime green leaves and beads in green and pastels.

Skill Level
Easy

Finished Size
Necklace: ½" × 19" (1.3 cm × 48.5 cm) with clasp
Earrings: 1¾" (4.5 cm) each with ear wire

Materials for Necklace and Earrings
- *Wire:* Artistic Wire, 28-gauge (40 yd [37 m] spool); 1 spool of black
- *Beads:* 1 tube (5 g) size 6° alabaster pearl beads
- *Hook:* Steel size 6/1.80 mm
- *Notions:* 1" (2.5 cm) sterling silver hook-and-eye clasp
2 silver fishhook ear wires
2 silver jump rings
Wire cutters
Chain-nose pliers

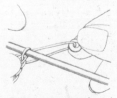 

Pull out about ¾" (2 cm) of wire with bead.
Twist wire with bead.

Necklace
Notes: String all beads on wire in random order.

To make a bead tendril: Bring bead up to about ¼" (6 mm) to ¾" (2 cm) from the crochet, fold the wire toward the back and next to the crochet. Vary the wire length with each bead you place. Hold the wire with the middle finger of your nondominant hand. Hold the bead with your dominant hand and twist until the bead is held tightly by the twisted wire. Be careful not to twist the wire too much or it will break.

Ch 4, sc in second ch from hook and in next 2 chs—3 sts.

Row 1: (RS) Make bead tendril, sc in first st, make bead tendril, keep on RS sc in second st, sc in last st.

Row 2: Make bead tendril, sc in first st, make bead tendril, move to RS, sc in second st, sc in last st, turn.

Repeat Rows 1 and 2 until necklace measures 18" (45.5 cm) or desired length. The beads will rest flat against the work as your hand passes over it to make the new rows.

You can move the beads if you like, but the random placement gives this necklace some of its charm.

FINISHING

Using the remaining wire ends, attach the jump rings of the clasp to the ends of the necklace. Weave in ends.

Earrings

Work as for necklace until 6 beads have been placed. Fasten off.

FINISHING

Using the remaining wire ends, attach the jump rungs in the loop at the top. Weave in ends.

ALTERNATIVE MATERIALS
Christmas

- *Wire:* Artistic Wire, 28-gauge (40 yd [37 m] spool); 1 spool of green
- *Beads:* 1 tube (5 g) size 6° mixed colors to look like Christmas lights

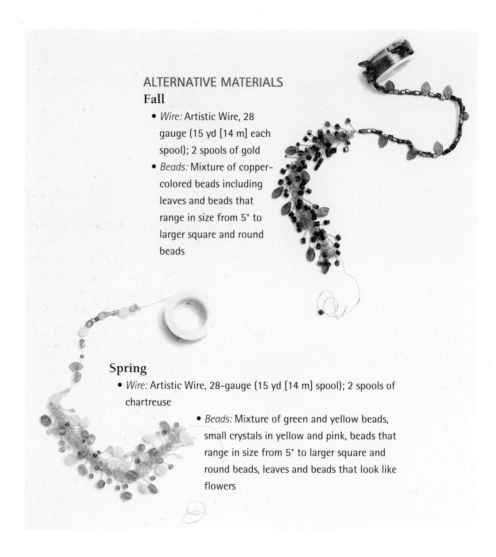

ALTERNATIVE MATERIALS
Fall

- *Wire:* Artistic Wire, 28 gauge (15 yd [14 m] each spool); 2 spools of gold
- *Beads:* Mixture of copper-colored beads including leaves and beads that range in size from 5° to larger square and round beads

Spring

- *Wire:* Artistic Wire, 28-gauge (15 yd [14 m] spool); 2 spools of chartreuse
- *Beads:* Mixture of green and yellow beads, small crystals in yellow and pink, beads that range in size from 5° to larger square and round beads, leaves and beads that look like flowers

Red Tube Necklace and Bracelet

To create this fabulous set, you'll work on these pieces "inside out" in the round. The combination of beads is up to you, and, of course, the color possibilities are endless.

Skill Level

Intermediate/Experienced

Finished Size

Necklace: ⅜" × 21½" (1 cm × 54.5 cm) with clasp

Bracelet: ⅜" × 8½" (1 cm × 21.5 cm) with clasp

Materials for Necklace and Bracelet

- *Wire:* Artistic Wire, 32-gauge (30 yd [28 m] spool); 1 spool of red
- *Beads:* 35 g mixed beads including:
  Size 6° and 8° seed beads
  Square beads and bugle beads ranging in color from dark pink through shades of red to dark purple
- *Hook:* Steel size 6/1.80 mm
- *Notions:* Silver clasps
Jump rings
Wire cutters
Chain-nose pliers

Necklace

Randomly string about 1¾ yd (1.6 m) of bead mixture on wire.

Notes: Always work on the inside of the tube. The beads will fall to the outside of the tube. Never join in rounds.

Ch 5, join with a sl st.

Row 1: (WS) Ch 1, sc with a bead in each ch around, do not join. You are working in a spiral.

All following rows: Insert hook under the bead for the next st from the previous row, push the bead over the hook to the right, sc a bead into the st.

Row 2: Sc a bead in each st around.

Rep Row 2 until necklace measures 20½" (52 cm) long. When the work measures 20" (51 cm), work one row without beads. Fasten off.

Insert hook under stitch with bead; move bead to the right.

Complete single crochet.

FINISHING

Attach clasp by inserting a jump ring into several layers of the crochet. Use chain-nose pliers to close the ring. Insert the remaining end of wire into the center of the piece and weave in. Finish off wire by working it into a bead and cutting close to the work.

TIPS AND HINTS:

- Every few rows count the number of beads in a round. If your bead count is off, either skip a stitch or increase a stitch to get back to 5 stitches per row.

- The bead you go under should be horizontal.

- Once a bead from a previous row has been crocheted it will look more vertical.

- At first, the piece will look flat; use the end of a knitting needle or pencil to push the center down and shape it into a tube.

- The thickness of the tube will vary from thin to thick depending on the size of the beads.

- If you need more beads, cut the wire leaving a 6" (15 mm) tail, string on more beads and begin crocheting again working over the tails and weaving them in securely. You can also tie a knot in the two ends of the wire.

Bracelet

String about 1¼ yards (1.6 m) of beads and work as for necklace. When the bracelet measures 7" (18 cm), work one row sc without beads. Fasten off. Finish as for necklace.

Choker and Bracelet with Flat Beads

Understated yet stunning, this design evokes a forest of fairy treasures woven among thin, soft vines. The flat beads make this set comfortable on the neck and arm.

Skill Level
Intermediate

Finished Size
Necklace: ⅜" × 15" (1 cm × 38 cm) with clasp

Bracelet: ½" × 7" (1.3 cm × 18 cm) with clasp

Materials for Necklace
- *Wire:* Artistic Wire, 28-gauge (15 yd [14 m] spool); 2 spools of olive
- *Beads:* ¼" (6mm) flat round beads to match wire, 168
- *Hook:* Steel size 3/2.10 mm
- *Notions:* Silver clasp

  Wire cutters

  Chain-nose pliers

Materials for Bracelet
- *Wire:* Artistic Wire, 28-gauge (15 yd [14 m] spool); 1 spool of olive (or leftovers from necklace)
- *Beads:* ¼" 6mm round beads, 47
- *Hook:* Steel size 3/2.10 mm
- *Notions:* Silver clasp

  Wire cutters

Necklace

String beads on wire.

(RS) Make a ch 16" (40.5 cm) long, chaining with a bead into each st, turn.

Row 1: (WS) Ch 1, working in front loop (FL) of sts, sc a bead in second ch from hook and in each ch across. Make sure all beads are on the RS.

Row 2: Ch 1. Turn. Sc a bead in each st using the top loop only of st. Make sure all beads are on the RS. Fasten off.

FINISHING

Sew on clasp with the remaining tails of wire on each end of the necklace. If necessary, sew an extra bead over the clasp to help hide it. Weave in ends, finishing off with a bead. Trim close to work.

Bracelet

String beads on wire.

Make a ch 6½" (16.5 cm) long, placing a bead into first ch, then every other ch; end with ch 1, turn.

Row 1: (RS) Make a ch 6½" (16.5 cm) long, chaining a bead into first st and then every other st; end with ch 1, turn.

Row 2: Sc in first st with bead, (sc bead into first ch 1 sp, sc into next st with bead). Repeat across row to last st, sc in last st with bead. Cut wire, finish off. Do not turn.

Row 3: With WS facing, go back to beg of Row 2; join wire with a sl st in first st, ch 1. Repeat Row 2. Cut wire; finish off.

FINISHING

Finish as for necklace.

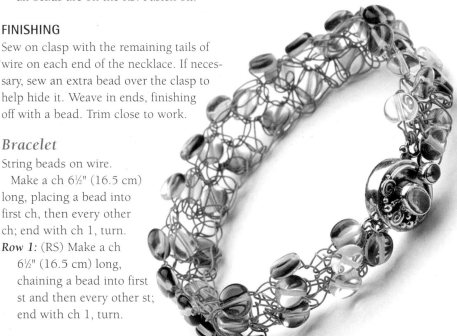

Seaweeds Necklace and Bracelet

Looking like gifts dredged from the depths of the ocean and threaded on bright seaweed, this necklace and bracelet combination can be adapted many ways. Shorter longer, more strands or fewer—the choices are endless as waves.

Skill Level
Beginner

Finished Size
Necklace: 24" (61 cm) with clasp
Bracelet: 8" (20.5 cm) with clasp

Materials for Necklace and Bracelet
- *Wire:* Artistic Wire, 30-gauge (15 yd [14 m] spool); 1 spool each of the following colors:
  Color A: peacock
  Color B: chartreuse
- *Beads:* 7 g mixed beads including:
  Size 6°, 8° seed beads
  Bugle beads to match color A wire
  3.5 g size 6° seed beads to match color B wire
  3.5 g size 8° seed beads in colors blended to match colors A and B wire
- *Hook:* Steel size 3/2.10 mm
- *Notions:* 2 gold lobster clasps
  4 jump rings
  Wire cutters

Necklace

Strand 1: Using color A, make a ch about 22" (56 cm) long, turn, sc in second ch from hook and in each st across. Fasten off.

Strand 2: Using color A wire, rep Strand 1, making it about 23" (58.5 cm) long. Fasten off.

Strands 3 and 4: Using color A, string mixed beads (to match) on wire. Make a ch about 24" (61 cm) long, crocheting a bead into each ch. Fasten off.

Strand 5: Using color A, string size 6° seed beads on wire. Make a ch about 22" (56 cm) long, ch a bead into each st. Fasten off.

Strand 6: Using color B, string mixed beads on wire. Make a ch about 23" (58.5 cm) long, ch a bead into each st. Fasten off.

Strand 7: Using color B, string size 8° seed beads on wire. Make a ch about 24" (61 cm) long, ch a bead into each st. Fasten off.

FINISHING

Lay all the strands out flat. Hold all the ends of the wire together at one end. Place a size 6° seed bead and a jump ring with the clasp over all the ends. Make a loop of wire over the center of the jump ring and push the

Jump ring placement—opposite end would have clasp.

ends back through the 6° seed bead. Wrap the ends around the base of the bead and secure. Rep for the other end with a size 6° bead, a jump ring and clasp.

Bracelet

Create Strands 3, 4, 5, 6, and 7 as given for necklace, making them about 7" (18 cm) long. Finish as for necklace and attach clasp.

Simply Sterling Necklace and Bracelet

Wearing pure silver is almost magical, and the wire is a dream to work with. You'll love this project, both the satisfaction of making the necklace and bracelet and showing them off.

Skill Level
Easy

Finished Size
Necklace: ¼" × 23½" (6 mm × 59.5 cm) with clasp
Bracelet: ¼" × 8" (6 mm × 20.5 cm) with clasp

Materials for Necklace and Bracelet
- *Wire:* 1 oz Rio Grande sterling silver wire, 28 gauge (40 yd [36.57 m])
- *Hook:* Steel size 2 (2.25 mm)
- *Notions:* ½" (1.3 cm) and ⅝" (1.5 cm) sterling silver lobster clasps
  4 sterling silver jump rings

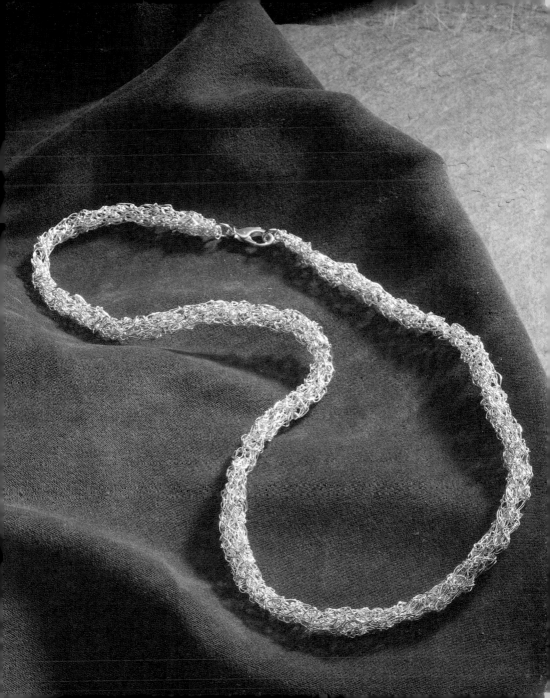

Necklace

Note: Always work on inside of tube.

Ch 4, join with a sl st in first ch.

Row 1: Ch 1, sc in each ch around, do not join. Working in a spiral with the tube toward the left, rotate it away from you, being careful not to crush the tube.

Row 2: Sc in each st around.

Row 3: Working in BL of sts, hdc in each st around.

There will appear to be a jump to the next row at the beg of every row. The tube will tend to flatten for the first few rows; push a knitting needle or pencil into the center to make the tube.

Rep Row 3 until tube measures 21½" (54.5 cm) long, work two rows of sc. Fasten off. Weave in ends in center of tube.

FINISHING

Insert jump ring into center of crochet at one end, then attach larger lobster claw to jump ring. Attach jump ring to other end.

Bracelet

Work as for necklace until tube measures 7½" (19 cm). Finish as for necklace with smaller lobster claw.

Gold Lace Necklace and Bracelet

Done in Tunisian stitch, this beautiful neck-lace and bracelet made of gold-filled wire are sure to become family jewelry heirlooms. The stitch is easy, but the results are enchanting with the solid inside look and the lacy edges. The gold-filled wire for this project is easy to work with, but you can substitute any Artistic Wire color if you desire.

Skill Level
Easy

Finished Size
Necklace: ⅝" × 18" (1.5 cm × 45.5 cm) with clasp
Bracelet: 1" × 8" (2.5 cm × 0.5 cm) with clasp

Materials for Necklace and Bracelet
- *Wire:* Master Wire Sculptor Wire, 28-gauge round dead-soft, gold-filled wire; 1 oz (28 g)
- *Hook:* Steel size 0 (3.25 mm)
- *Notions:* Gold hook clasp for necklace
  Gold toggle clasp for bracelet
  Wire cutters

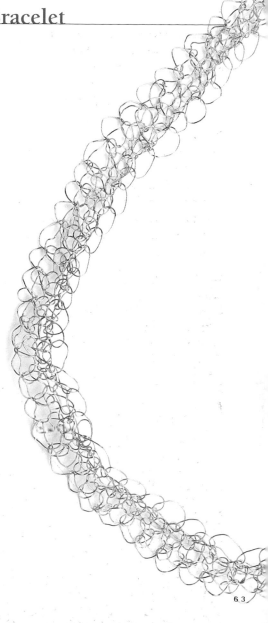

Necklace

Set-up Row: Ch 4, sk 1 ch, 1 sc in next 3 chs, turn.

Row 1: (Insert hook in next st, pull up a loop) 3 times. Four loops on hook. Do not turn. (Yoh, pull through two loops) 3 times. Do not turn.

Row 2: (Insert hook into vertical wire created by last row) 3 times. Note that this includes last loop. There are now four loops on hook. (Yoh, pull through 2 loops) 3 times. Do not turn.

Repeat Row 2 until necklace measures 18" (45.5 cm). Fasten off.

FINISHING

Use crochet hook to pull out loops on both edges. Roll gently with rolling pin. Sew on hook clasp with tails of wire on each end. Weave in ends of wire and fasten off.

Bracelet

Ch 6

Row 1: (Insert hook in next st, pull up a loop) 5 times. Note that this includes last loop. There are now six loops on hook. Do not turn. (Yoh, pull through two loops) 5 times. Do not turn.

Row 2: (Insert hook into vertical wire created by last row) 5 times. Six loops on hook. Note this includes last loop. (Yoh, pull through two loops) 6 times. One loop on hook. Do not turn. Rep Row 2 until bracelet measures 6¾" (17 cm). Fasten off.

FINISHING

Sew on toggle clasp with tails of wire at each end. Weave in ends, fasten off.

Zigzag Necklace and Bracelet

Remember the old zigzag or ripple pattern used to crochet afghans? My mother used to make those afghans by the dozens. Here is an updated wire version made into a necklace and bracelet that are very different from the traditional use of the pattern, and a whole lot more fun.

Necklace

String 18 crystals on wire. Ch 5, ch 1 with crystal, (ch 9, ch 1 with crystal) 8 times, ch 6—9 crystals used. Turn.

Row 1: Ch 1, 2 sc in second ch from hook, *1 sc in next 3 ch, sk 2 ch (includes ch over crystal), 1 sc in next 3 ch, 3 sc in next ch ; repeat from * until 4 sts rem. 1 sc in next 3 ch, 2 sc in last ch, turn.

Row 2: Ch 1, 2 sc in second sc from hook, *1 sc in next 3 sc, sk 2 sc, 1 sc in next 3 sc, 3 sc in next sc; repeat from * until 4 sts rem. 1 sc in next 3 sc, 2 sc in last sc.

Row 3: Ch 1, 2 sc in first sc, *sc in each of next 3 sc, sk 2 sc, sc in each of next 3 sc, sc in next sc, sc with bead in same sc, sc in same sc; rep from * until 4 sts rem, sc in each of next 3 sc, 2 sc in last sc. *At the end of Row 3:* Ch 20, slide a crystal up to the hook, turn, sc in each ch of ch 20 just made, sl st in last st of Row 3. Fasten off.

Skill Level

Intermediate

Size

Necklace: 1¼" × 15½" (3.2 cm × 39.5 cm) with clasp

Bracelet: 1½" × 7¾" (3.8 cm × 19.5 cm) with clasp

Materials for Necklace

- *Wire:* Artistic Wire, 28-gauge (15 yd [14 m] spool); 2 spools of plum
- *Beads:* 18 crystals, 6mm, to match wire
- *Hook:* Steel size 4/2.00 mm

- *Notions:* ¾" (2 cm) silver or pewter hook clasp
  Wire cutters
  Chain-nose pliers

Materials for Bracelet

- *Wire:* Artistic Wire, 28-gauge (15 yd [14 m] spool); 2 spools of plum
- *Beads:* 11 crystals, 6mm, to match wire
- *Hook:* Steel size 4/2.00 mm
- *Notions:* Pewter hinged clasp
  Wire cutters

FINISHING

Thread the hook for the closure on the wire, reattach wire to the other end of necklace, ch 5, slide the hook up to the crochet hook, turn, sc in each ch of ch 5 just made. Fasten off.

Bracelet

String 11 crystals on wire. Ch 5, bring a crystal up close to hook, (ch 9, bring a crystal up close to hook) 5 times, ch 6, turn—6 crystals used.

Row 1: Rep Row 1 of necklace.

Rows 2–4: Rep Row 2 of necklace (3 times).

Row 5: Rep 3 of necklace with crystals placed as directed. Fasten off.

FINISHING

Attach clasp.

Filet Crochet Necklace and Bracelet

I love filet crochet (also called double cro-chet). This necklace and bracelet set is easy to create with filet crochet in a simple grid pattern that makes natural places to add velvet ribbons . . . but you could add leather or lace.

Necklace

Row 1: Ch 9, dc in third ch from hook, dc in each ch across, turn—8 sts.

Row 2: Ch 2 (counts as first dc), dc in each of next 2 sts, ch 2, sk next 2 sts, dc in each of last 3 sts, turn.

Row 3: Ch 2, dc in each st across, turn.

Rep Rows 2 and 3 until piece measure about 13½" (34.5 cm); end with Row 3. Fasten off.

Skill Level

Easy

Finished Size

Necklace: ⅞" × 14½" (2.2 cm × 37 cm) with clasp

Bracelet: 1⅜" × 7" (3.5 cm × 18 cm) with clasp

Materials for Necklace

- *Wire:* Artistic Wire, 30-gauge (30 yd [28 m] spool); 1 spool of gold
- *Hook:* Steel size 8 (1.50 mm)
- *Notions:* ½" (1.3 cm) gold filigree square box clasp 18" (45.5 cm) ⅜" (1 cm) black velvet ribbon

FINISHING

Weave velvet ribbon through the holes created by Row 2. Cut ribbon, leaving 1½" (3.8 cm) at each end. Fold ¼" (6 mm) hem in each end of the ribbon and fold again. Sew hem to the end of the wire necklace on the wrong side; be sure to catch the wire of the necklace as you sew. Sew one end of the clasp to the fold in the ribbon. Rep for other side.

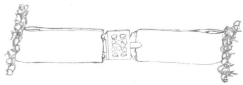

Clasp sewn to velvet.

Sewing thread to match velvet ribbon

Sewing needle

Wire cutters

Materials for Bracelet

- *Wire:* Artistic Wire, 30- gauge (30 yd [28 m] spool); 1 spool of gold
- *Hook:* Steel size 8 (1.50 mm)
- *Notions:* ½" (1.3 cm) gold filigree square box clasp 10" (25.5 cm) ⅜" (1 cm) black velvet ribbon

Sewing thread to match velvet ribbon

Sewing needle

Wire cutters

Bracelet

Row 1: Ch 14, 1 dc in third ch from hook, dc in each of next 2 sts, ch 2 sk next 2 ch, dc in each of next 3 ch) twice, turn—13 sts.

Row 2: Ch 2 (counts as first dc), dc in each of next 2 sts, 3 dc in next ch-2 sp, ch 2, skip 3 dc, 3 dc in next ch-2 sp, dc in each of last 3 dc, turn—14 sts.

Row 3: Ch 2 (counts as first dc), dc in each of next 2 dc, ch 2, sk 3 dc, 3 dc in next ch-2 sp ch 2, dc in each of last 3 dc, turn—13 sts.

Repeat Rows 2 and 3 until bracelet measures 6" (15 cm), end with Row 3.

FINISHING

Finish as for necklace, cutting the ribbon ¾" (2 cm) at each end for finishing.

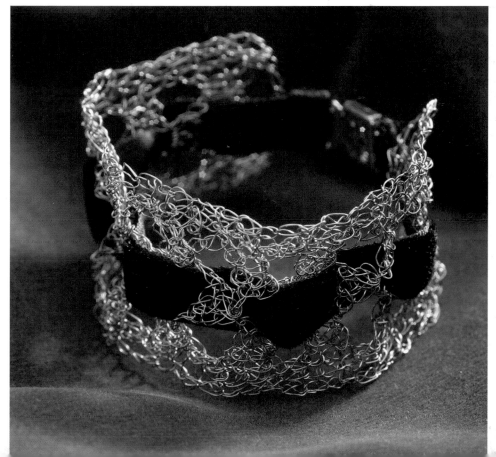

Granny Square Purse

I'll bet Grandma never thought she'd see her favorite crochet square worked up in wire! This charming little purse is just perfect for a night out or for a cute everyday coin purse. And it's great for using up wire scraps— Grandma would approve.

MAKE 2

Note: Ch 2 at beg of row counts as a dc.
   Using color A wire, ch 4, join with a sl st in first ch.
Rnd 1: (RS) Ch 2, 2 dc in ring (ch 1, 3 dc in ring) 3 times, ch 1, join with a sl st in turning ch. Cut wire, fasten off.

Rnd 2: With RS facing, join color B in any ch-1 sp with a sl st, (ch 2, 2 dc, ch 1, 3 dc) in same ch-1 sp, ch 2, (3 dc, ch 1, 3 dc, ch 2) in each next ch-1 sp around, join with a sl st in turning ch. Cut wire, fasten off. There are now four corners made of (3 dc, ch 1, 3 dc).
Rnd 3: With RS facing, join color C in ch-1 sp of any corner with a sl st, (ch 2, 2 dc, ch 1, 3 dc) in same ch-1 sp, ch 2 (3 dc in next ch-2 sp (side), ch 2, *(3 dc, ch 1, 3 dc) in next ch-1 corner sp, ch 2; rep from * twice, 3 dc in next ch-2 sp, ch 2, join with a sl st in turning ch. Cut wire, fasten off.

Skill level
Intermediate

Finished Size
3½" (9 cm) square

Materials
- *Wire:* Artistic Wire, 30-gauge (15 yd [14 m] spool); 1 spool each of the following colors:
  Color A: silver
  Color B: plum
  Color C: aqua

- *Hook:* Steel crochet hook size 6 (1.80 mm)
- *Notions:* 3½" (9 cm) wide silver purse frame (sample uses #BL 950S from Bag Lady)
  1 yd (.9 m) silver rope chain (sample uses #C2S with two 6-mm split rings to attach chain to purse frame)
  3½" × 7" (9 × 18 cm) piece of lining fabric
  Sewing thread
  Sewing needle
  Optional: Sewing machine for seams (may be hand sewn)
  Wire cutters

Rnd 4: With RS facing, join color A in ch-1 sp of any corner with a sl st, (ch 2, 2 dc, ch 1, 3 dc) in same ch-1 sp, *ch 2, (3 dc, ch 2) in each of next 2 ch-2 spaces, (3 dc, ch 1, 3 dc) in next ch-1 corner sp; rep from * twice, ch 2, (3 dc, ch 2) in each of next 2 ch-2 spaces, join with a sl st in turning ch. Cut wire, fasten off.

Rnd 5: With RS facing, join color B in ch-1 sp of any corner, (ch 2, 2 dc ch 1, 3 dc) in same ch-1 sp, *ch 2, (3 dc, ch 2) in each of next 3 ch-2 spaces, (3 dc, ch 1, 3 dc) in next ch-1 corner sp; rep from * twice, ch 2, (3 dc, ch 2) in each of next 3 ch-2 spaces, join with a sl st in turning ch. Cut wire, fasten off.

FINISHING

Using color B, sew top half of two sides and the top edge of one granny square through the holes on one side of the purse frame. Rep for other side (be sure side edges of granny squares match). Whipstitch side seams and bottom edge of granny squares together with color B, matching sts.

LINING

Zigzag or overcast all edges of fabric to prevent fraying. Fold fabric in half with RS together to make a 3¼" (8.5 cm) square. Using a ¼" (6 mm) seam allowance and leaving the top half open, sew a 1¾" (4.5 cm) seam starting at the bottom on each side seam. Turn the lining right-side out and press. Clip the corners, fold a ¼" (6 mm) hem toward the right side on the remaining edges, press, and machine sew the hem. Insert the lining with the right side against the wrong side of the granny squares. Sew the lining with sewing thread to the purse frame through the same holes you used to sew the granny squares to the purse frame.

Attach the rope chain to the loops on top of the purse frame with the split rings.

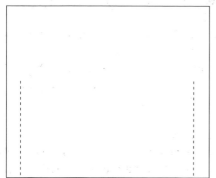

Purse lining inside out; 1¾" (4.5 cm) seam.

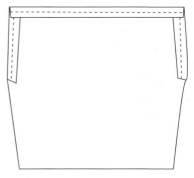

Stitching around upper edge of purse lining right side out.

Squares and Triangles Basket

This unusual project starts out as small pieces crocheted in squares and triangles that are then sewn together to make an interesting basket sculpture. Investigate the many ways you can use these simple shapes to make different baskets—or create a piece of art that expresses your individuality!

Skill Level

Intermediate

Finished Size

3½" (9 cm) square

Materials

- *Wire:* Artistic Wire, 26-gauge (15 yd [14 m] spool) in the following amounts and colors:
  3 spools Color A: blue
  2 spools Color B: green
  2 spools Color C: silvered lilac
  2 spools Color D: silvered rose
  3 spools Color E: plum
- *Hook:* Steel size E
- *Notions:* Rolling pin
  Wire cutters

BOTTOM

Using color A wire, ch 17.

Row 1: Hdc in second ch from hook, hdc in each ch across, turn—16 sts.

Rows 2–9: Hdc in each st across. Finish off, set aside.

SQUARES

Make 2 in color A, 3 each in colors B and D, 2 each in colors C and E.

Ch 9.

Row 1: Hdc in second ch from hook, hdc in each ch across, turn—8 sts.

Rows 2–4: Ch 2, hdc in each st across, turn. Finish off, set aside.

TRIANGLES

Make 1 each in colors B, C, D, and E.

Ch 9.

Row 1: Sc in second ch from hook, sc in each ch across, turn—8 sts.

Rows 2–7: Ch 1, sk first st, sc in each st across, ch 1, turn—1 st remains in last row. Finish off. Set aside.

FINISHING

To block the pieces, roll each one with a rolling pin on a hard surface. Be sure to roll from top to bottom in the direction of the crochet.

Using the diagram as a guide, whipstitch the pieces for the bottom row to the base. Start with Side 1 and work around to Side 4. After sewing the pieces to the bottom, whipstitch the sides of the squares together. Leave the triangles loose on top.

Starting at Side 1 again, whipstitch the second row of pieces to the top of the bottom row. The top of each triangle will be sewn to the middle of the square above it. When that row is completed, sew the sides of the squares tog, again leaving the triangles loose on the top.

TOP EDGING

Rnd 1: With RS facing, starting at the corner between Sides 1 and 2, and using color E, work around top edge of box as follows: For each square, work 8 sc across the top edge; for each triangle, ch 3, sc in the top of the triangle, ch 3. Join with a sl st in first sc at the beg.

Rnd 2: Ch 1, sc in each st around, join with a sl st in first sc. Fasten off.

Pinch each corner to make the edging square.

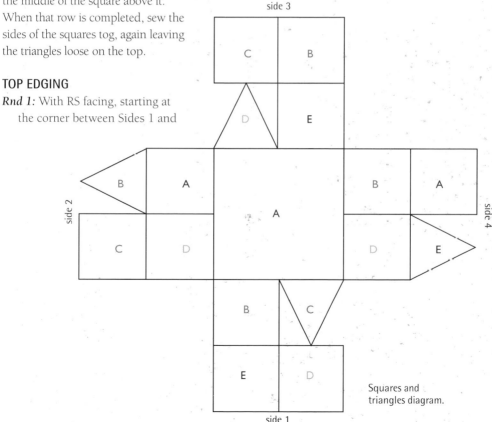

Squares and triangles diagram.

Pot O' Gold

Skill level
Intermediate

Finished Size
Bottom: 2" (5 cm) in diameter

Top: 3½" (9 cm) in diameter

Height: 1½" (3.8 cm)

Materials
- *Wire:* Artistic Wire, 28-gauge (15 yd [14 m] spool); 2 spools of gold
- *Hook:* Steel size E/3.50 mm

Note: Work with the inside of the basket facing you. Never turn the work at the end of a row.

Holding little pastel candies or a place card, this sweet little basket would be perfect on the dining table at a spring party. Make it in any of the colors that 28-gauge wire comes in and you'll treasure it for a long time.

Ch 4, join with a sl st in first ch.

Rnd 1: (WS) Ch 1, 2 sc in each ch around, join with a sl st—8 sts.

Rnds 2 and 3: Ch 1, 2 sc in each st around—32 sts in last rnd.

Rnds 4–7: Ch 2 (counts as first dc), dc in back loop (BL) of each st around, join with a sl st in turning ch.

Rnd 8: Ch 2 (counts as first dc), dc in first st, * 2 dc in next st, dc in next st; rep from * around, join with a sl st in turning ch—48 sts. Fasten off.

FINISHING
Weave wire ends into crochet. Gently pull on the last row worked to flare it out. Shape the basket in your hand so it sits flat.

Two-wire Basket

This is a simple single crochet basket with increases at both ends to give it an oval shape. The magic is that you crochet over a heavy wire so the basket maintains its size and stands up on its own. It can be adapted into a larger size without any problem. Have fun!

Using copper wire, ch 8.

Rnd 1: Holding the magenta wire over the copper wire and leaving about a 1" (2.5 cm) tail, work 1 sc in second ch from hook over the magenta wire and in next 6 ch across; work 3 sc in last ch. Curve the magenta wire around the end of the original ch and, working into the back loops of the original ch, sc over the magenta wire in the next 6 sts, work 3 sc in last ch, do not join. Work in a spiral, continuing in rounds as follows: Ch in each st around, working 3 increases in the center st at each end, always working over the magenta wire until bottom measures 3½" (9 cm) at its widest point. Continue as established working 2 sc in the center st at each end. Work until bottom measures 4½" (11.5 cm) at widest point.

Skill Level

Intermediate

Finished Size

4¼" long × 2" wide × 2" deep
(11 cm × 5 cm × 5 cm)

Materials

- *Wire:* Artistic Wire, 30-gauge (30 yd [28 m] spool); 1 spool of copper 20-gauge (15 yd [14 m] spool): 1 spool of magenta
- *Hook:* Steel size 1 (2.75 mm)
- Notions: Wire cutters

Notes: You will crochet the copper wire over the heavier magenta wire. Doing so will require manipulating the magenta wire into the oval shape of the basket as you work. Do not let the magenta wire get too tight or the basket will be too small. Pull on the magenta wire and shape it into an oval as you crochet with the copper wire. When you complete a round, pull out on the edges where you've made the increases to allow the magenta wire to fill in and make the basket as large as the single crochet will allow.

SIDES

Work even in sc without further increases until side measures 2" (5 cm) deep. On the last row, work to middle of long edge, cut magenta wire leaving ½" (1.3 cm) tail. Continue to crochet with copper wire over the end of the magenta wire until covered. Fasten off copper wire. Weave in end of copper wire. Fasten off inside tail of magenta wire by folding it back against itself and trimming to about ½" (1.3 cm).

Hold heavier wire to the left and over the st as you crochet a new stitch.

Triangular Trinket Box

Here's a charming triangular crochet box whose added beads make it extra special. Use it to hold jewelry, candy, or any other tiny treasures. It's a great gift, too.

Skill Level
Intermediate

Finished Size
4" (10 cm) across each side by 2" (5 cm) deep

Materials
- *Wire:* Artistic Wire, 28-gauge (15 yd [14 m] spool); 2 spools of tangerine
- *Beads:* 150 gold red-lined, size 5° triangular beads
- *Hooks:* Steel sizes 2 (2.2 mm) and 3 (2.10 mm)
- *Notions:* Wire cutters

Using size 2 (2.2 mm) hook, ch 22.

Row 1: (RS) Sc in second ch from hook, sc in each ch across, turn—21 sts.

Rows 2—22: Ch 1, sk 1 st, sc in each st across—1 st rem in last row. Cut wire, Fasten off.

SIDES

Row 1: With RS facing on one edge of bottom, join wire with a sl st at right corner, ch 1, sc evenly across edge to next corner, turn.

Rows 2–5: Ch 1, sc in each st across, turn— 22 sts. Fasten off.

Rep for remaining two edges.

Fold the sides on the edges where the sts were picked up and whipstitch the side seams together with wire.

BEAD EDGINGS

Side edgings: String beads on wire. Using size 3 (2.10 mm) crochet hook, join wire at one corner junction between two sides, ch 1; working through double thickness and pinching the corners, work a row of sc per bead with each st down side seam. Rep on each corner side seam.

Top edge: With wrong sides facing, join wire with a sl st in any corner on top edge, ch 1, sc with a bead into every other st around top edge. Fasten off.

Bottom edge: With bottom facing, join wire with a sl st in any corner on bottom edge, sc a bead into every other st around bottom edge. Fasten off.

FINISHING

Weave ends of wire into a few beads and cut close to work.

Abbreviations

beg	begin/beginning	RS	right side
BL	back loop	sc	single crochet
ch st	chain stitch	sk	skip
cont	continue	sl st	slip stitch
dc	double crochet	sp	space
FL	front loop	st(s)	stitch(es)
foll	following	tbl	through back loop
hdc	half double crochet	WS	wrong side
rem	remain/remaining	yoh	yarn over hook
rep	repeat		

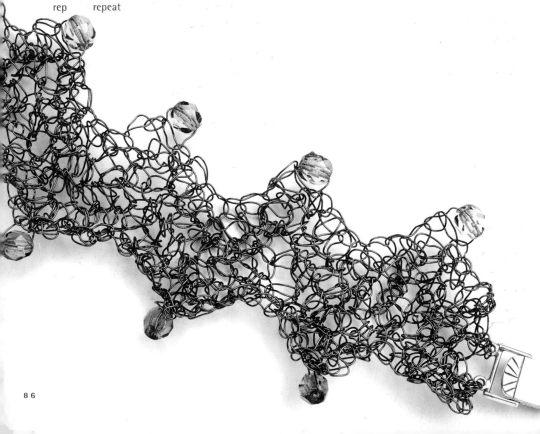

Resources

Artistic Wire
752 North Larch Ave.
Elmhurst, IL 60126
(630) 530-7567; fax (630) 530-7536
www.artisticwire.com

Bag Lady
PO Box 2409
Evergreen, CO 80437-2409
www.baglady.com

Fire Mountain Gems and Beads
One Fire Mountain Wy.
Grants Pass, OR 97526-2373
(800) 355-2137
www.firemountaingems.com

Master Wire Sculptor, LLC
1600 Clay St.
Vicksburg, MS 39183
(877) 636-2137
www.wire-sculpture.com
For gold wire

Rio Grande
7500 Bluewater Rd. NW
Albuquerque, NM 87121-1962
(800) 545-6566; fax (800) 965-2329
www.riogrande.com

Rishashay
300 Evans
Missoula, MT 59801
(800) 517-3311
www.rishashay.com

Bibliography

Brown, Nancy. *Crocheter's Companion*. Loveland, Colorado: Interweave Press, 2002.

Kooler, Donna. *Encyclopedia of Crochet*. Little Rock, Arkansas: Leisure Arts, 2002.

Wiseman, Nancie M. *Knitting with Wire*. Loveland, Colorado: Interweave Press, 2003.

Index